Stained Glass
Windows of Distinction

Featuring
McMow Art Glass
STUDIO DESIGNERS

Collection One

D1451223

Wardell
PUBLICATIONS INC.

PREFACE

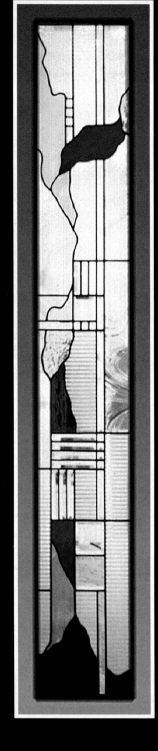

We would like to welcome everyone to the design world of McMow Art Glass Inc. We have been designing and fabricating stained glass windows since 1976. Over the years we have had the privilege of creating windows for a diverse and eclectic group of individuals. Some of our clients have given us the opportunity to open our minds and take our art into new avenues. Many of these designs are included in this collection. Hopefully you will experience the result of our imagination set free to transform what would normally be mere glass openings into unique grand entryways.

We here at McMow Art Glass Inc. sincerely hope that this book will be an inspiration to architects, builders, interior designers and art glass enthusiasts alike. We strongly encourage you to "open your minds" and "set your imaginations free" to explore for yourself and your clients the advantage of clearly outstanding window designs.

Shanon & Phil Materio

This book is dedicated to the memory of Frank Materio,
who let us dream our own dream.
"Although the world may scoff and jest
... a life of service is the best" – F.M.

McMow Art Glass Inc. is located in Lake Worth, Florida. USA

Copyright © 1995 by
Wardell Publications Inc.

Cataloging in Publication Data

McMow Art Glass Inc.
   Stained Glass Windows of Distinction, Collection One
ISBN 0-919985-22-X

1. Glass painting and staining - Patterns - Catalogs.
2. Glass craft - Patterns - Catalogs.
3. McMow Art Glass Inc. - Catalogs. I. Title

TT298.M36 1995   748.5'022'2   C95-931247-1

Stained Glass
Windows *of* Distinction
Collection One

DESIGNERS

EXECUTIVE DESIGNER
Shanon Materio
SENIOR DESIGNER
Marilyn Ford
ASSOCIATE DESIGNERS
Anita Balboni Ricardo Drummond

FABRICATION

PRODUCTION MANAGER
Phil Materio

& McMow Staff Associates

PHOTOGRAPHY

Ping Dai Carlos Dominish Phil Materio Randy Wardell
Cover photo & pages 1, 25, 29, 33 & 37 by Kim Sargent

GENERAL EDITOR

Randy Wardell

GRAPHICS & TYPOGRAPHY

Randy Wardell

SPECIAL THANKS

To Leza Hepler who keeps us all together. To Joyce Corwin for her beveling skills which are highlighted throughout this book. To Joe & Dee Silvestri who keep our other lives in order. To Flora Materio and Richard Materio for their unwavering support. To Marian and Ed Adamko for just being there. To John & Tiffany Boswell who set the artist free in us all. To Jeanette, Taylor, & P.J. our best creations. And finally, to all the customers and friends that these pages reflect.

PRINTED IN CANADA
by Thorn Press Ltd.

PUBLISHED BY

Wardell
PUBLICATIONS INC.

Some Important Information

Window Sizes and Drawing Scale

All of the line drawings in this book were carefully drawn to 10% of full-size, normally referred to as a 1" = 10" or 1 cm = 10 cm scale. If you were to enlarge the drawings to 10 times their present size they would be accurate to the full size dimensions listed with each drawing.

The color photographs are not presented in any particular scale and no dimensions are listed. The photographs were sized to give the maximum possible viewing advantage. You may find a photograph of a single door panel beside a photo of a complete entryway, both may be printed at a similar size, but the entryway would be many times larger in reality.

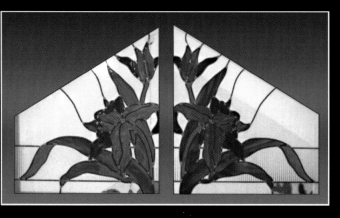

Full-size Drawings.

The designs in this book are not available commercially as full-size drawings. The intent of this book is to present proposal drawings and color photographs of stained glass windows for inspiration and enjoyment. You can use these designs exactly as they are presented or use any portion of them or alter them in any way you wish. The dimensions listed with the drawings are there to give you a feeling for the size of the window. While the drawings could be enlarged exactly as they are presented, it is unlikely that your particular instal-lation will be exactly the same dimensions as those listed. It is best to use these drawings and photographs as a foundation to build your design on, taking the parts and pieces of each that meet your requirements.

Stock Bevels:

Over half of designs in this book use bevels to one degree or another. Most of these windows make use of standard "stock" bevel widths and whenever possible the designs also use standard "stock" lengths as well. However, in order to fit the window into a specific frame dimension it is frequently necessary to cut a stock bevel shorter or cut it at an angle, then re-bevel the ends that were cut.

An excellent way to cut down on custom beveling charges is to use stock bevel strips. These are longer length bevels, usually 24" (60.9cm) long for the 1" (2.5cm) wide to 36" (91.4cm) or 48" (121.9cm) long for the 1-1/2" (3.8cm), 2" (5.1cm), 3" (76.2cm) and 4" (101.6cm) wide bevel strips. (lengths will vary among manufacturers). Simply use the appropriate width strip and cut it to fit the required length, then bevel the ends with your own beveling machine or send it out to a beveling service to be finished.

Custom Bevels:

While it is true that most of the designs in this book make use of standard "stock" bevel sizes, it is also true that a good number of them require some custom bevel sizes and shapes. If you do not have your own beveling equipment you will need to use a custom beveling service. (local glass supply retailers usually have a custom bevel ordering service). Custom bevels are priced by the total inches (or cm's) of beveling required, usually a higher price is charged for curved beveling than for straight line beveling. Simply cut a full-size paper pattern of the bevel shape you want and send it to the beveling service and they will return the completed bevel to you. Some services will charge less if you to send a bevel blank (the bevel shape cut out from the thicker plate glass material) and some will use your customized "stock" bevels and re-bevel only the areas that were cut to shape. However, the savings may not be worth it if you need to ship the blanks a distance away to the beveling service. Ask for prices and do some calculations before you start cutting up a lot of stock bevels.

Section Contents & Style Locator

This locator is loosely structured on the style as indicated by the section title.
Some window designs fit into two or more of these section definitions.
Please use this contents page as a sampler guide only.

Section One - Geometric Designs

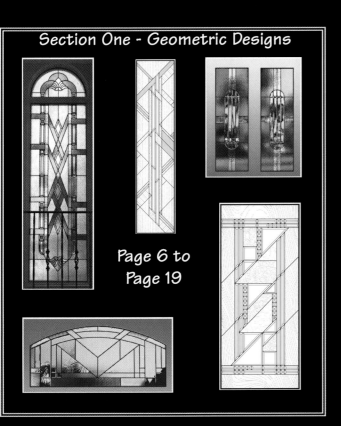

Page 6 to
Page 19

Section Two - Grand Entryways

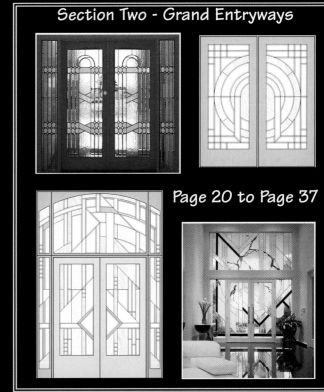

Page 20 to Page 37

Section Three - Nouveau Nature

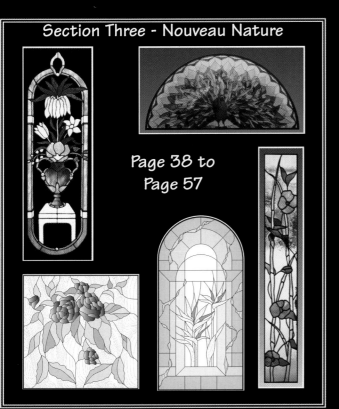

Page 38 to
Page 57

Section Four - Abstractions

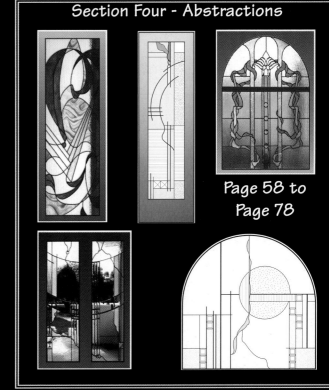

Page 58 to
Page 78

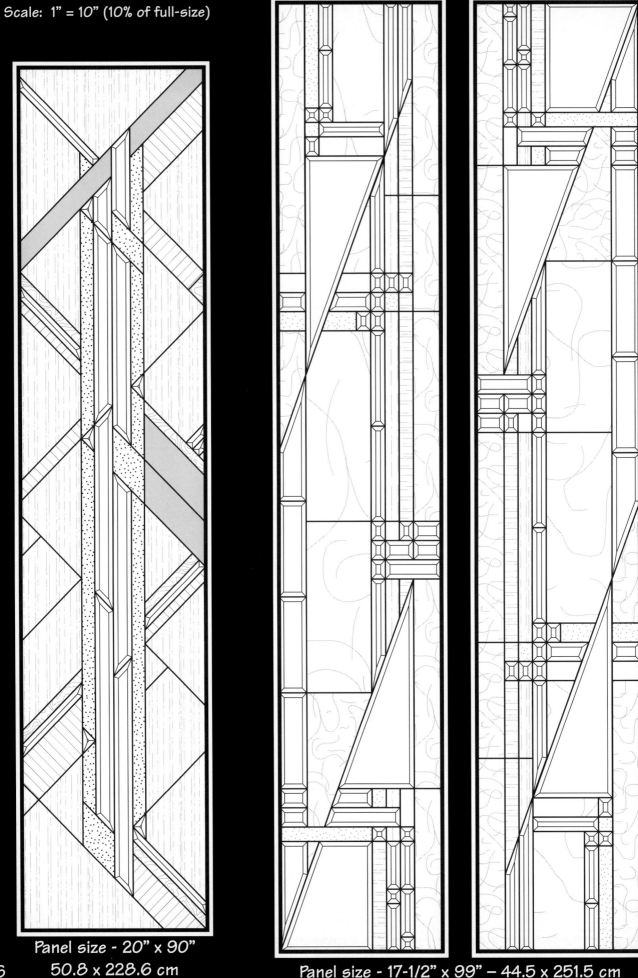

Scale: 1" = 10" (10% of full-size)

Panel size - 20" x 90"
50.8 x 228.6 cm

6

Panel size - 17-1/2" x 99" – 44.5 x 251.5 cm

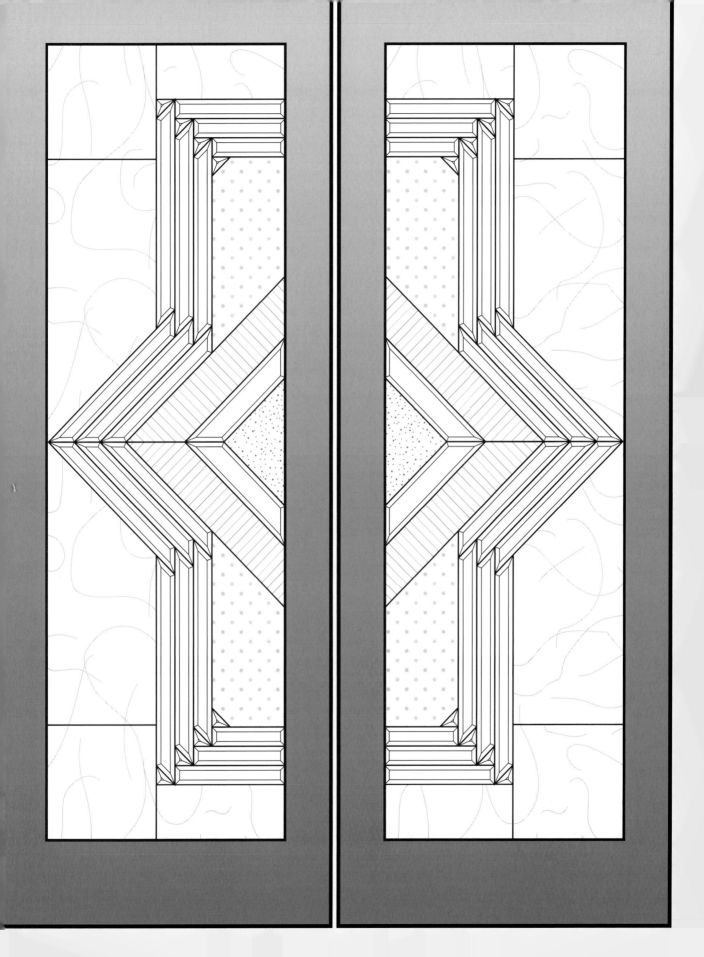

"Whenever possible we like to use stock bevels and bevel strips, then do some minor beveling adjustments to create affordable and elegant beveled entryways" - S.M.

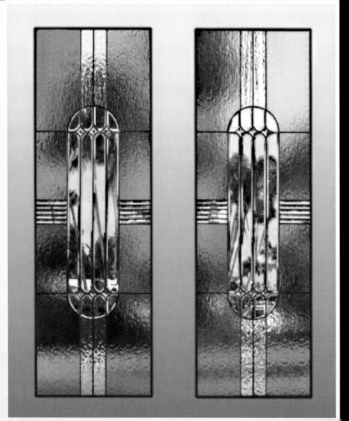

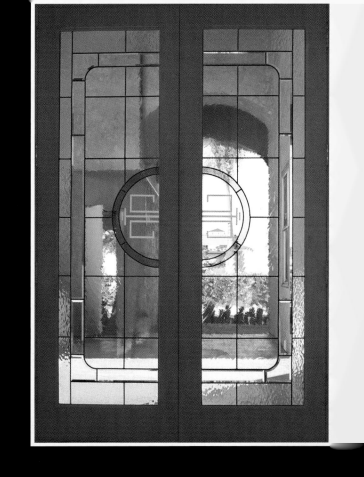

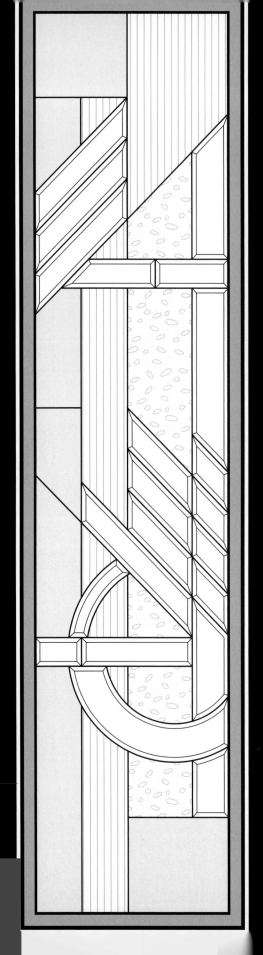
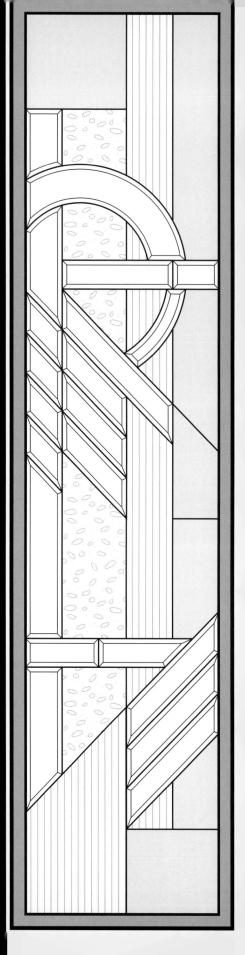

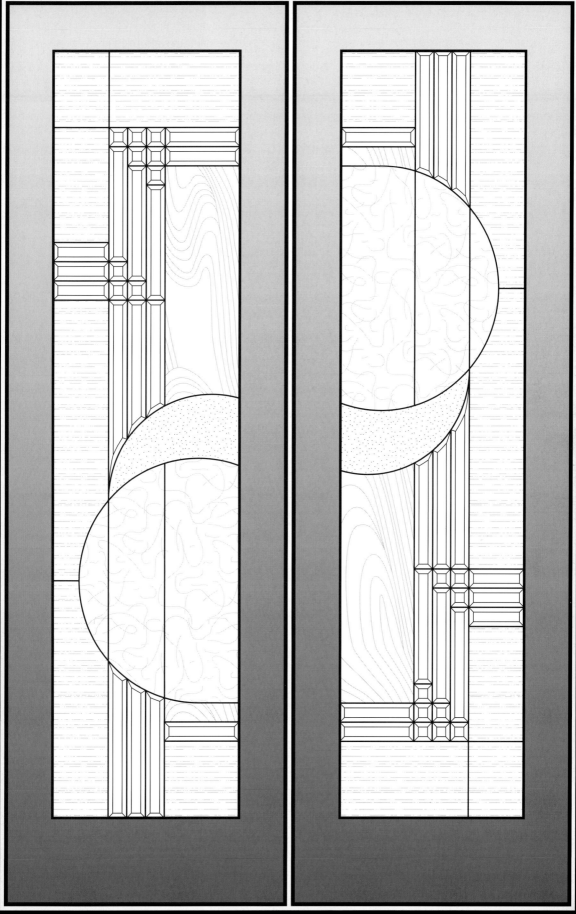

Door Panel size - 20" x 80" – 50.8 x 203.2 cm

"Simply changing glass choices to clear textures can create a more contemporary design" - S.M.

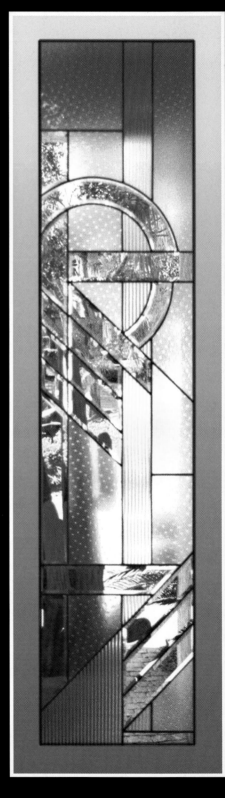

"If 10 designers selected the glass for the same window, you'd get 10 very different looking designs; your choice of glass makes all the difference." - M.F.

Door Panel size - 18-1/2" x 58" – 47 x 147.3 cm

"Often a simple bevel cluster or stock bevel combination makes the most elegant design" - M.F.

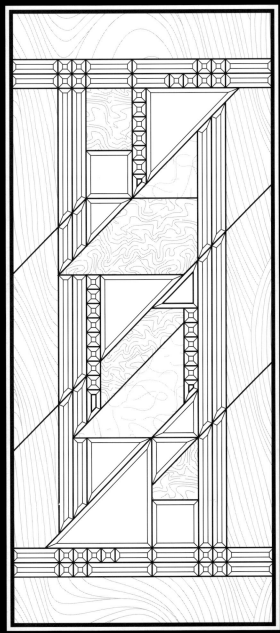

Panel size - 28" x 64" – 71.1 x 162.6 cm

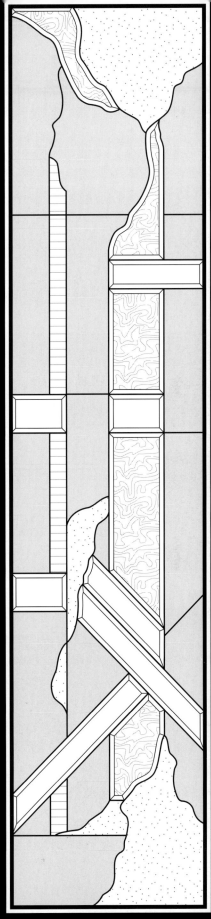

Panel size - 21" x 94" – 53.3 x 238.7 cm

Scale: 1" = 10" (10% of full-size)

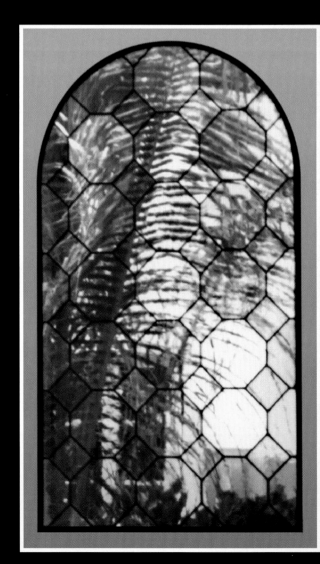

"A lot of people comment about how this entrance has a southwestern flair" - S.M.

The designs on these two pages are simple, elegant entryways, yet very dramatic" - M.F.

Door Panel size - 23-3/4" x 70-3/4" – 59.7 x 179.7 cm

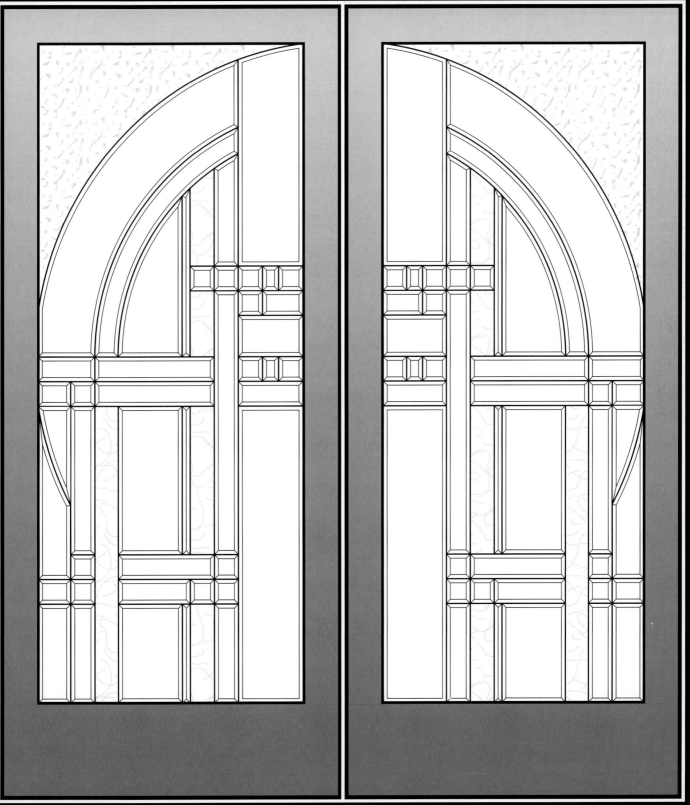

Door Panel size - 28-3/8" x 68-3/4" – 72.1 x 174.6 cm

Turn to the back cover for a color photograph of of these panels.

Scale: 1" = 10" (10% of full-size)

"We were very excited about how well the combination of bevels, clear text-ures and etched glass worked in this entry." - P.M.

"This grand entry is another example of our extensive use of
stock bevel strips combined with custom bevels" - M.F.

"This entryway was inspired by the design of the iron gate installed at our client's residence" - M.F.

Door Panel size - 26" x 64-1/4" 66 x 163.2 cm

"This design is an abstraction of ocean waves, inspired by our south Florida beach location" - S.M.

This was designed for the front entry of my analyst's home—
So tell me, how does this design make you feel?" - S.M.

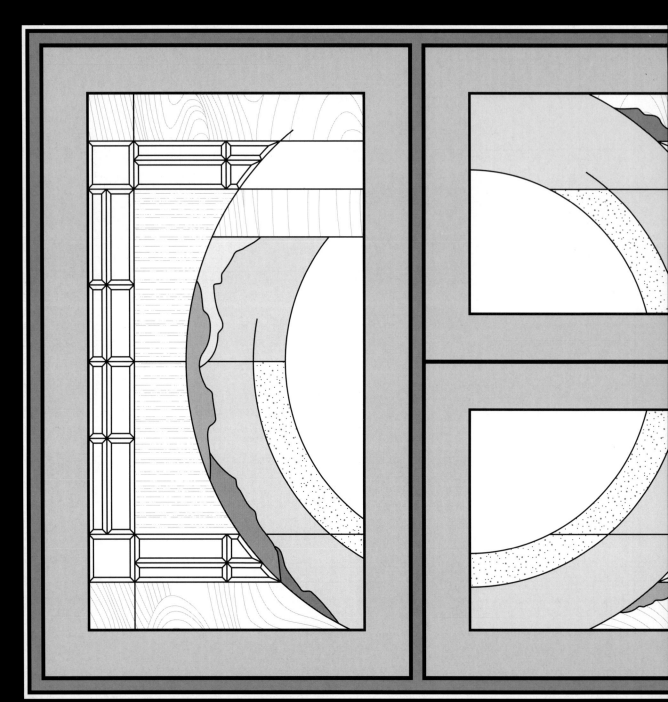

Transom Panel size - 56" x 30" – 142.2 x 76.2 cm

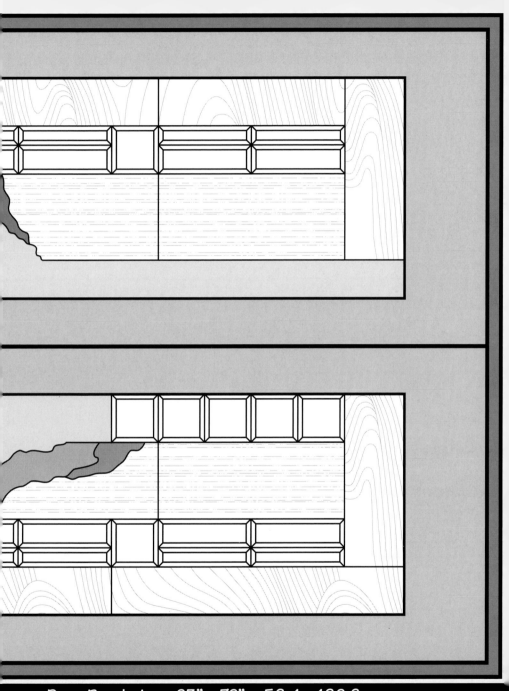

Door Panel size - 23" x 72" – 58.4 x 182.8 cm

Entryway size (including frame) - 66" x 127" – 167.6 x 332.6 cm

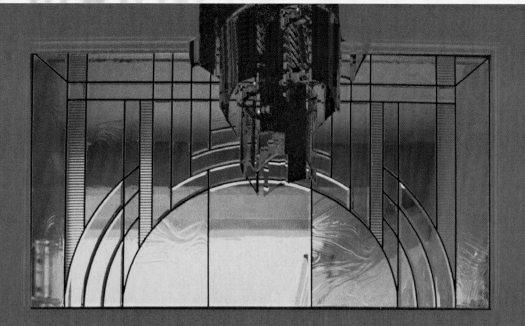

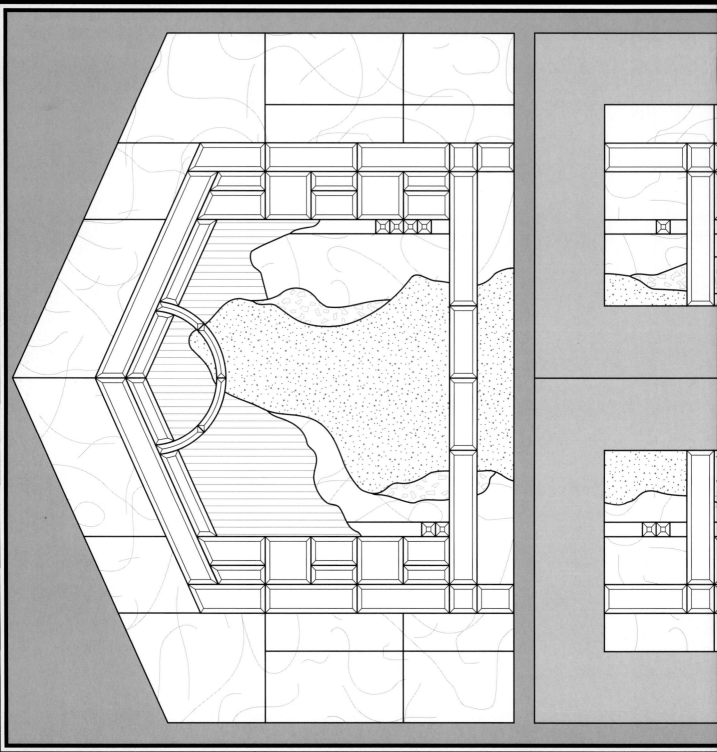

Transom Panel size - 54-1/2" x 72" – 138.4 x 182.8 cm

Scale: 1" = 10" / 1 cm = 10 cm (10% of full-size)

Turn to page 32 to see a color photograph of the completed entryway.

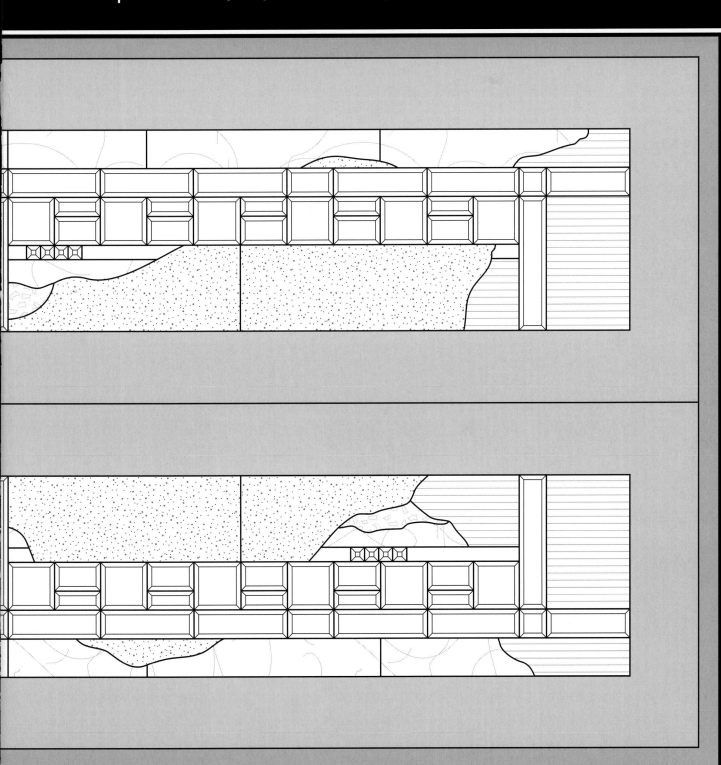

or Panel size - 21" x 79" — 50.4 x 200.6 cmm&

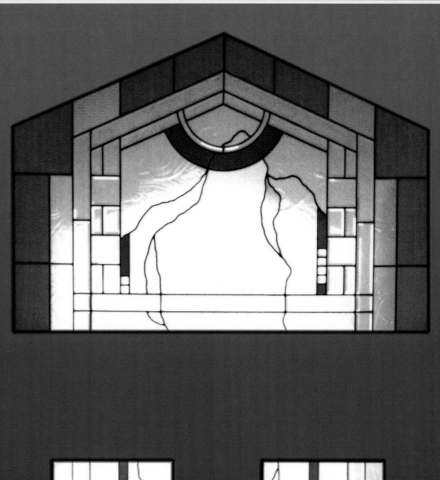

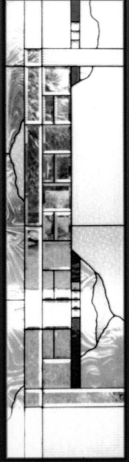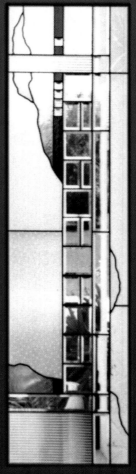

"Many people tell us how much they like the way we placed the bird in this window. This is our most famous design fluke; and it works" - S.M.

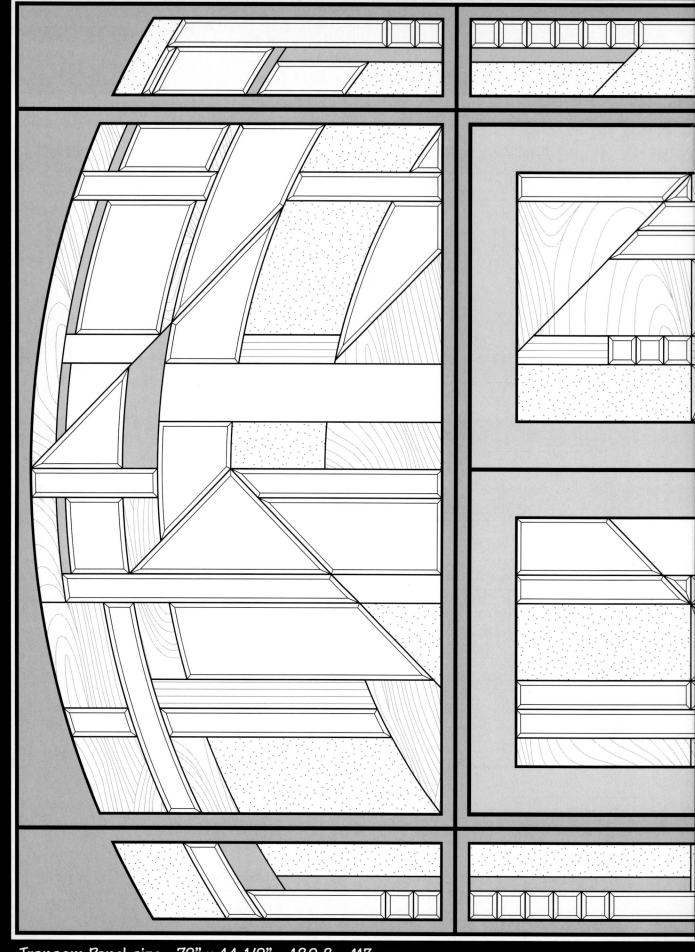

Transom Panel size - 72" x 44-1/2" – 182.8 x 113 cm
Transom Sidelite size - 8" x 35-1/2" – 20.3 x 90.2 cm

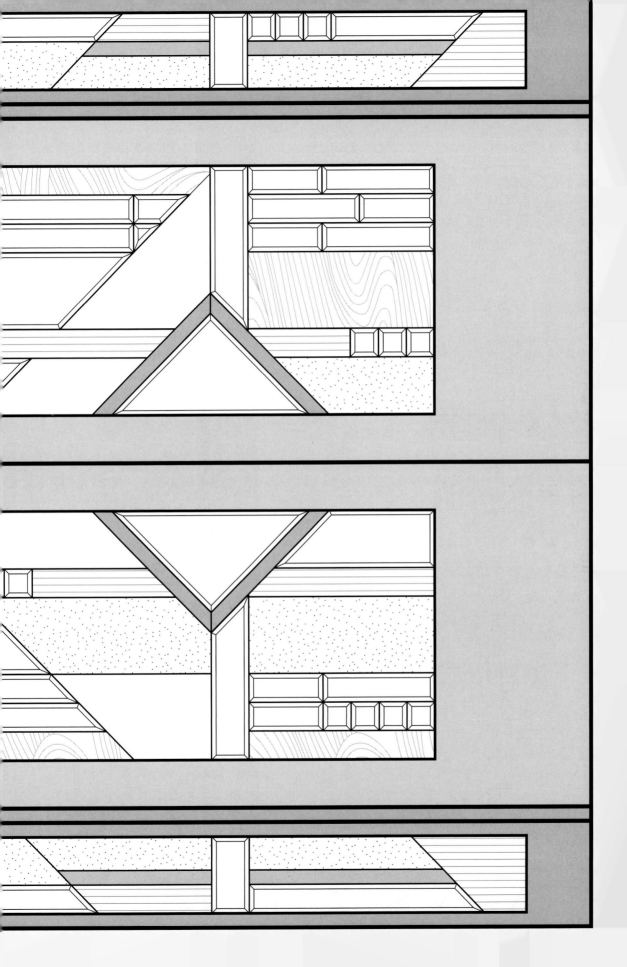

"This entryway was created for an optometrist, any reference to eye glasses is purely accidental" - S.M.

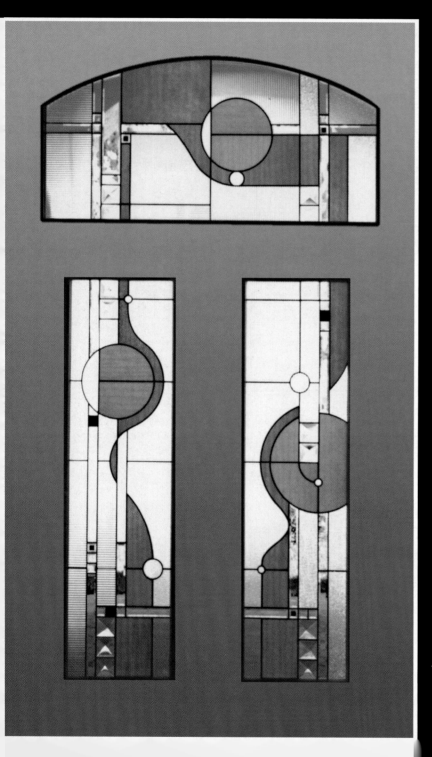

This entryway is awesome in person, we used all mouth blown antiques & opaque antiques; it's very sophisticated without being pretentious" - S.M.

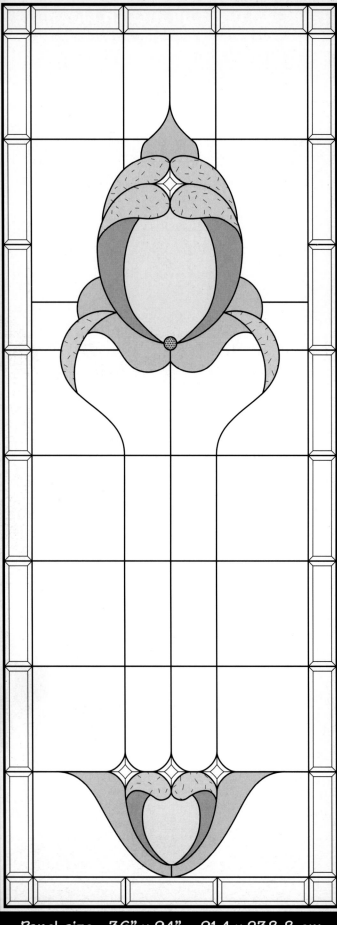

Panel size - 36" x 94" – 91.4 x 238.8 cm

"This pair of master suite doors (opposite page) uses all custom bevels. We think it is both elegant and romantic and it's one of my favorites." - M.F.

A photograph of a sister design is on page 40.

Panel size - 28"x 67" – 71.1 x 170.2 cm

"From simple to sophisticated nothing says it like flowers" S.M.

Panel size - 61-3/4" x 59" – 156.8 x 149.8 cm

Panel size - 32" x 72" – 81.3 x 182.8 cm

"This is not homage to Louis Comfort but rather to one of our favorite clients" - S.M

45

Panel size - 48" x 89" – 121.9 x 226.1 cm

Panel size - 19-1/2" x 35"
49.5 x 88.9 cm

Panel size - 19" x 53"
48.3 x 134.6 cm

"I love to be inspired by nature and a lot of my designs reflect this interest with floral & fauna influences." -A.B.

Panel size - 36" x 74" - 91.4 x 188 cm

Panel size - 36" x 82-3/4 - 91.4 x 210.2 cm

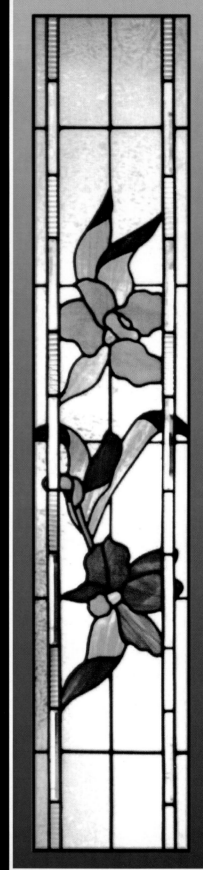

48

"Flowers and birds give us a chance to put some vibrant colors into our windows" -S.M.

49

"This is not a
typical tropical
design, We have
even used this
bird of paradise
as inspiration for
a grand entry-
way" - S.M.

Turn to page 37
to see a color
photograph of
the entryway.

Panel size - 45" x 90" – 114.3 x 228.6 cm

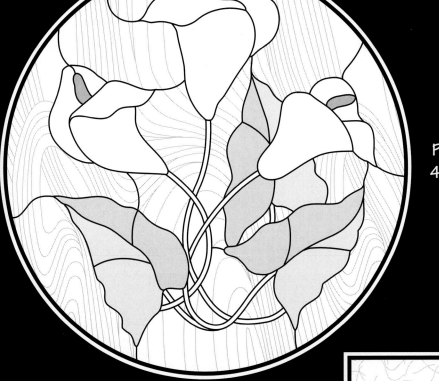

Panel Diameter
43" – 109.2 cm

"The two little girls were thrilled to be used as models for this design. I really like the sense of fun and freedom that is suggested by the floating ribbons" - M.F.

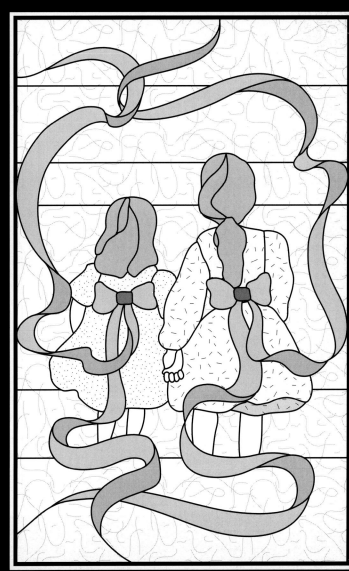

Panel size - 36" x 57"
91.4 x 144.8 cm

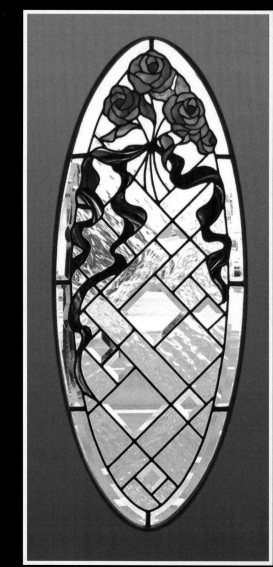

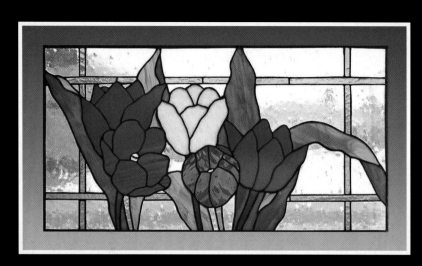

"Our clients depend on us to maintain a creative diversity"-M.F.

Scale: 1" = 10" (10% of full-size)

Overall Entryway size (including frame) - 67-1/4" x 94-3/4" — 170.8 x 240.7 cm

Overall Entryway size (including frame) - 76-1/2" x 94-1/2" – 194.3 x 240 cm

"Here you can see the impact that living in the tropical south has on many of our designs" - S.M.

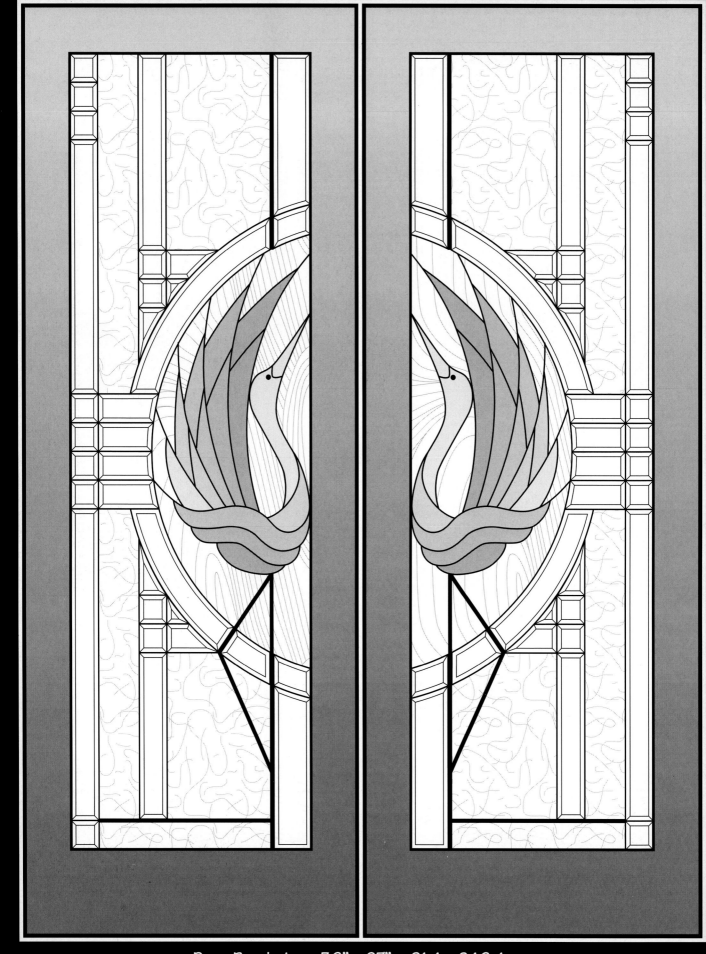

Door Panel size - 36" x 97" – 91.4 x 246.4 cm

Turn to page 12 to see a color photograph of this entryway.

Panel size - 30" x 54" – 76.2 x 137.2 cm

Panel size - 30" x 54" – 76.2 x 137.2 cm

Turn to page 16 to see a color photograph of one of this panel.

Panel size - 7" x 18"
17.8 x 45.7 cm

Panel size - 7" x 18"
17.8 x 45.7 cm

Scale: 1" = 10" / 1 cm = 10 cm (10% of full-size)

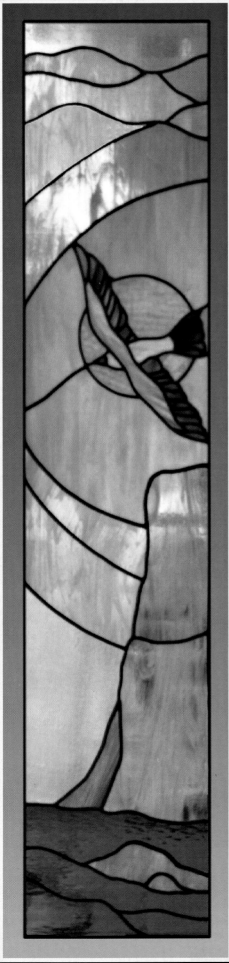

"We used real seashells in this underwater scene" - S.M.

Door Panel size - 25-5/8" x 82" – 65.1 x 208.3 cm

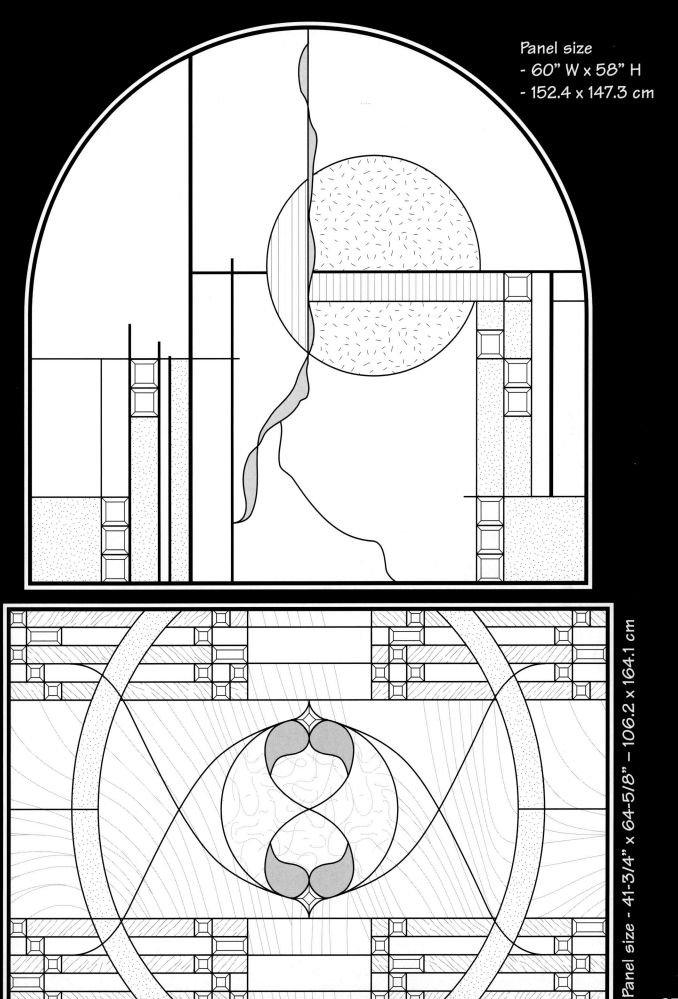

Panel size
- 60" W x 58" H
- 152.4 x 147.3 cm

Panel size - 41-3/4" x 64-5/8" – 106.2 x 164.1 cm

63

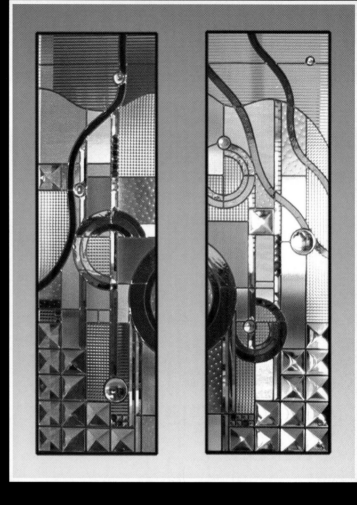

"We love these funky whimsical designs and many of our clients do as well. " -S.M.

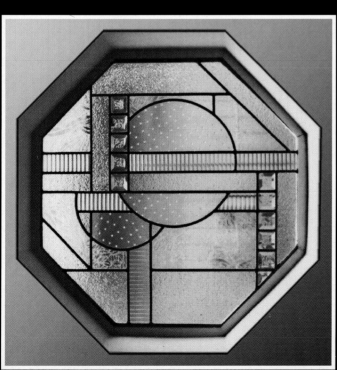

Door Panel size - 23" x 72" – 58.4 x 182.9 cm

Turn to page 69 to see a color photograph of these french doors.

Door Panel size - 20" x 86" – 50.8 x 218.4 cm

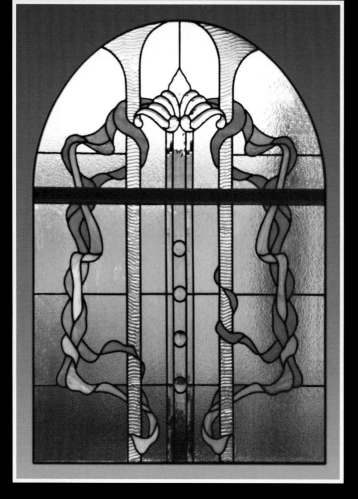

"Abstract designs are not always sharp angles and straight lines" -M.F

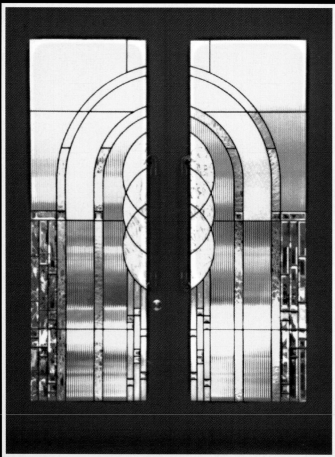

69

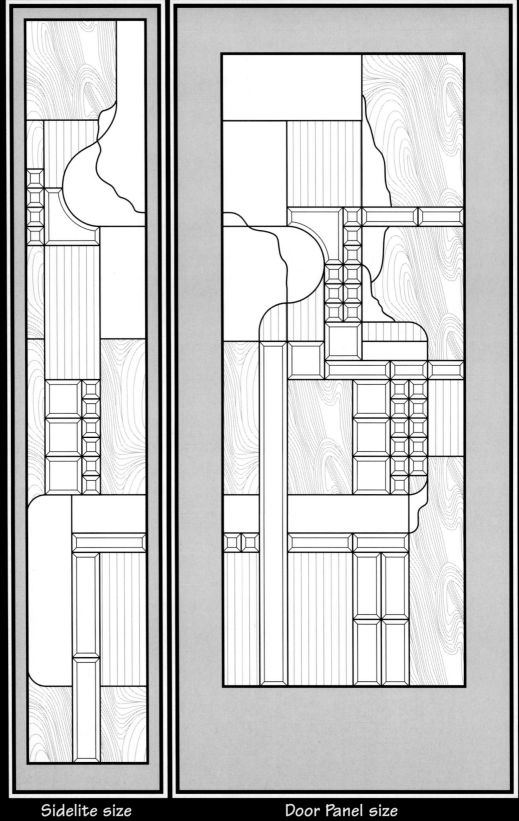

Sidelite size
13" x 77-1/2"
33 x 196.8 cm

Door Panel size
26" x 66"
66 x 167.6 cm

Scale: 1" = 10" / 1 cm = 10 cm (10% of

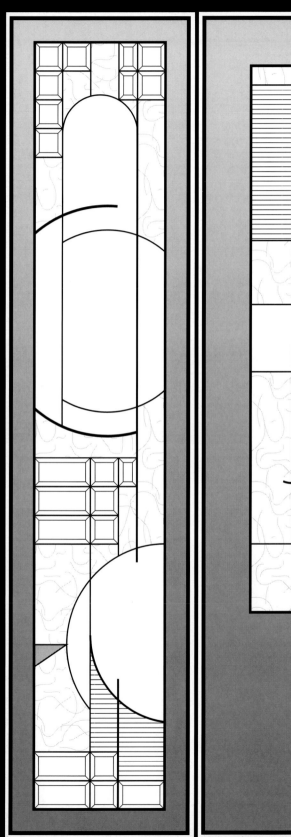

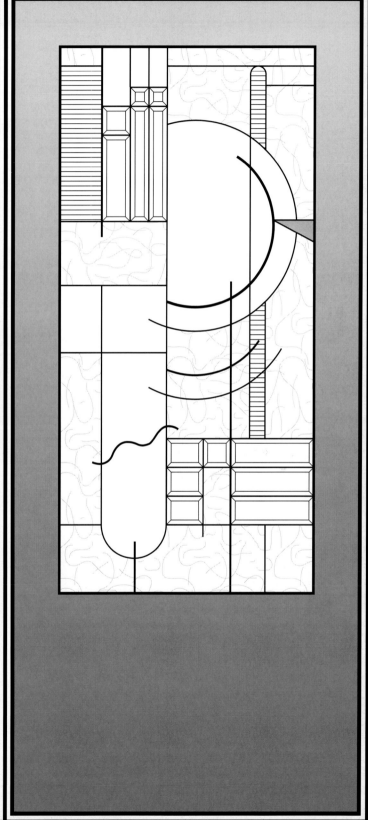

Sidelite size

Door Panel size

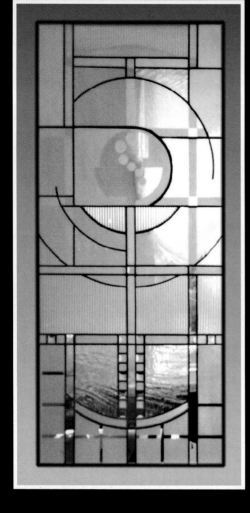

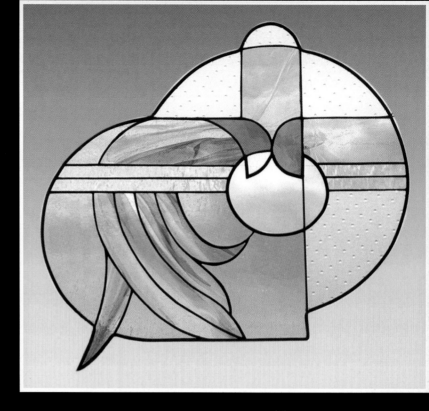

"Sometimes we just let our imaginations go wild" - S.M.

"Lots of color or no color at all – don't be afraid to break away and experiment" -S.M.

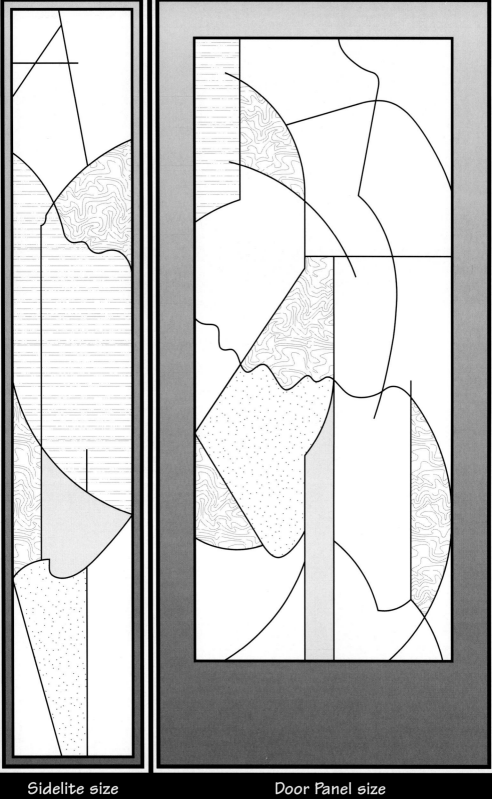

Sidelite size
13" x 78"
33 x 198.1 cm

Door Panel size
28" x 65"
71.1 x 165.1 cm

"We used very wide lead and extensions to add "visual strength" S.M

Turn to page 77 to see a color photograph of a similar design.

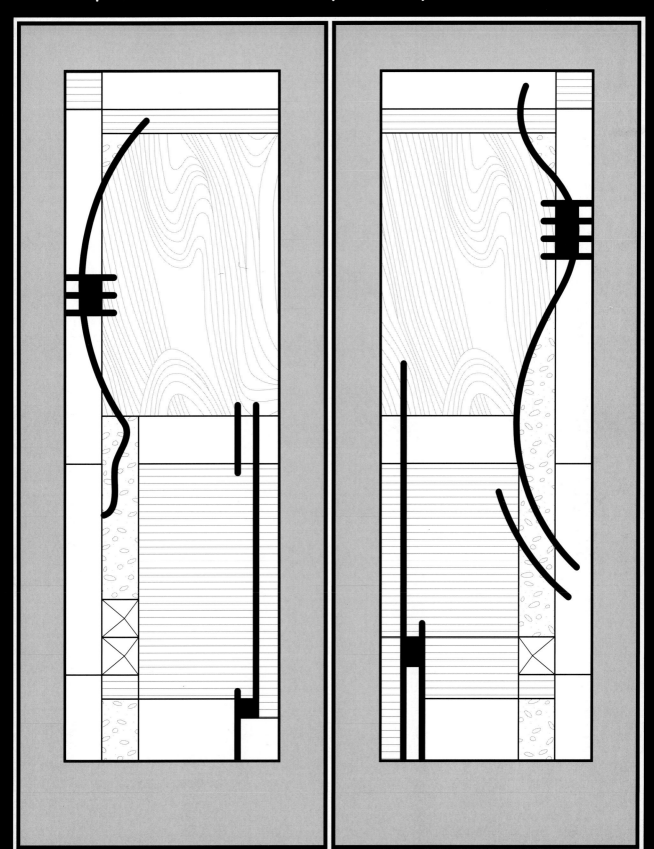

Door Panel size - 23" x 72" — 58.4 x 182.9 cm

"For some reason designing in this linear style is natural and effortless for me" M.F.

"These abstract linear designs are a kind of signature of our art department. We really enjoy using bevels and glass textures in this way. -S.M.

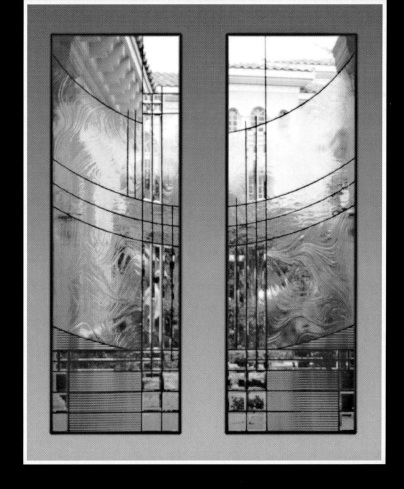

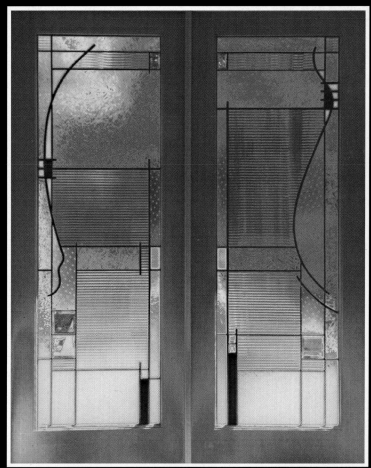

"Here is another one of our lead gone crazy designs. We would suggest keeping the glass textures subtle, and allow the lead lines to carry the design."
- S.M.

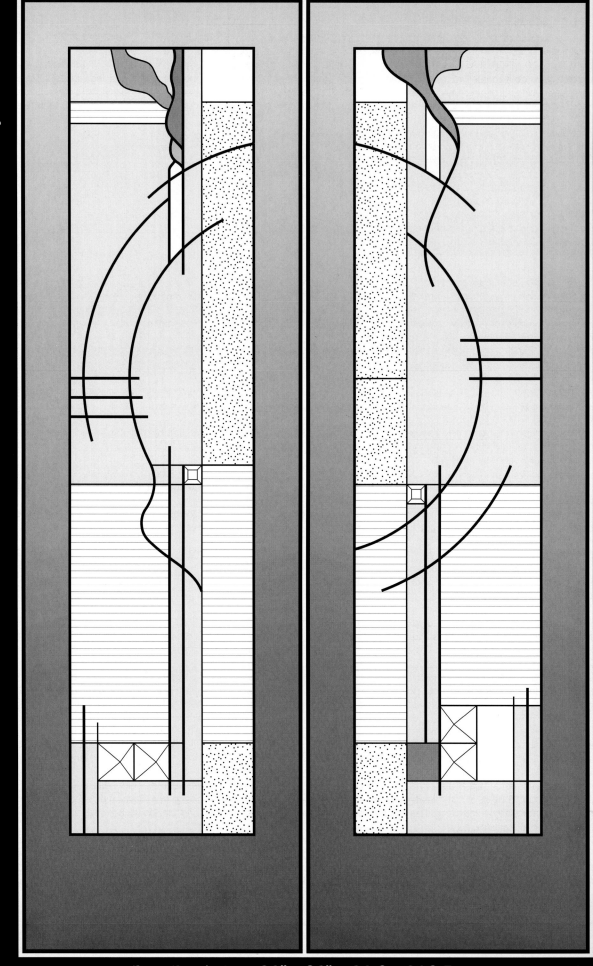

Door Panel size - 20" x 82" – 20.8 x 208.3 cm

The Wardell Publications Stained Glass Library

QUICK SUCCESS STAINED GLASS by Wardell   48 pages   18 Patterns

This all color instruction book is designed to get new crafters up and running as quickly as possible. The quick read format makes learning stained glass craft techniques simple and fun. 18 full-size patterns. Detailed safety guides throughout the book.

INTRODUCTION TO STAINED GLASS by Wardell   70 pages   17 Patterns

A comprehensive do-it-yourself manual providing in-depth step-by-step information on tools, supplies and techniques. Instructions include pattern making, glass cutting, fitting, soldering, and finishing for both copper foil and lead came assembly. Lamp making and other special techniques are also covered. 17 project patterns are included ranging from sun-catchers, boxes and small windows to stained glass swag & table lampshades.

LAMPSHADE PATTERNS I by Wardell   48 pages   22 Patterns

Full-size patterns for 22 shades ranging in diameter from 5" to 16". All are shown in color, matched with an appropriate lampbase. Included is an instruction guide with trade secrets to guide all crafters in 3 dimensional lampshade assembly.

MORE LAMPSHADE PATTERNS II by Wardell   28 pages   11 Patterns

Step-by-step instructions and full-size patterns for 11 large swag-style shades. The designs include six dining room lamps (16" to 22") a 15" x 27" pool table lamp and four (14" to 19") living room styles. All projects shown in full color.

DESIGNS FOR LAMPS by C. Knapp   48 pages   18 Patterns

An exciting collection of full-size patterns for 18 lampshades from 6" to 15" in diameter. These shades were designed primarily to be mounted on a lampbase and information to help match the base to shade is provided.

LAMPWORKS by 5 designers   46 pages   16 Patterns

Lamp patterns, by five different designers, include 3 inverted ceiling lampshades, 4 table-lamps and 9 swag lamps. Some incorporate bevels and for a challenge, an elaborate 24" diameter old rose dining room lamp. Assembly instructions included.

NORTHERN SHADES by 6 designers   46 pages   25 Patterns

The 25 full-size lampshade designs range from small night-stand styles, to elaborate dining room show pieces. Included are 3 wall sconces, which are convertible to medium swag shades for matching lamp sets. You will also find 2 of the popular inverted ceiling style shades. Most shades are medium sized, suitable for either swag or lampbase applications. Color photographs and instructions

BEVEL ART LAMPSHADES by C. Knapp   46 pages   29 Patterns

29 full-size lampshade designs in this book range from small night-stand styles, elaborate dining room swags, wall sconces with matching swag lamps, plus 3 of the popular inverted Torchiere style shades, this book offers every crafter and all studios a lampshade pattern for virtually any location.

STAINED GLASS BOXES by Wardell   68 pages   34 Patterns

34 patterns for the popular stained glass jewelry box. The design styles include a sailboat, antique car, geometrics, mini ring boxes & a storage box for audio cassettes. The simple assembly steps are fully explained and all boxes are shown in color.

TERRARIUMS & PLANTERS by Wardell   68 pages   30 Patterns

This comprehensive book contains a wide range of designs for 30 plant containers. The step-by-step assembly instructions are accompanied by a helpful guide to selecting and caring for plants in terrariums. All projects are photographed in color.

WALL DECORATIONS by Wardell   68 pages   29 Patterns

This book contains 29 patterns for assorted clocks, mirrors & picture frames. Projects include a 30" high granddaughter clock, 11", 22" & 29" oval mirrors, a pendulum schoolhouse clock and much more. All are shown in color with instructions.

BEVEL WINDOW DESIGNS - 2nd Edition by Wardell   72 pages   114 Drawings

This book has 32 color photographs and over 100 detailed line drawings of beveled glass windows offering a broad range of design styles including traditional, floral, birds, landscapes, and much more. How-to methods for pattern enlarging, custom designing, framing and more. A book of inspirations.

CLASSIC ALPHABETS by T. Martin   48 pages   8 Patterns

This book contains three complete alphabet styles and two numeral styles. There are 20 line drawings of project ideas for use in traditional stained glass or sand-etching. Information on creating a full-size drawing, dividing the background and use of color. 8 full-size patterns for signs, frames, a planter, etc.

MIRRORS & FRAMES by Wardell   52 pages   43 Patterns

27 full-size patterns for mirror frames, plus 16 glass overlay designs which can be combined in an almost countless number of ways. The extensive instruction section includes information on working with mirror glass, adjusting patterns, sealing the mirror edge and important tips for preventing "creeping black edge". All projects are photographed in color and have a specification & material list.

CLOCK GALLERY by Wardell   52 pages   18 Patterns

A stained glass book dedicated to clocks. Patterns include a 31" high grandfather clock, a school house regulator plus several floral wall-mounted & traditional free-standing clocks. The how-to section has valuable information on clock movement installation, metal clock faces, bezels and pendulum bob adjustments. All projects are shown in color & are complete with specification and material lists.

ART GLASS INSPIRATIONS by S. CANN   42 pages   32 Patterns

32 Free-form designs for window lightners of sports figures, pets, flowers and birds plus 5 fan lamp designs. An exciting feature of the designs in this collection is the surface paint effects. An extensive how-to section explains the simple painting technique using a special transfer paper that is included with the book. All projects are photographed in color and have a specification & material list and an estimated time to complete.

WINDOWS OF DISTINCTION by McMow Art Glass Designers   80 pages   110 Color photographs   45 Drawings

This book contains more than 150 stained glass window designs. The collection is drawn from the studio designer's portfolio of McMow Art Glass covering more than 18 years of commissions. Styles include all aspects of leaded glass design from beveled panels to landscape but the spectacular entryways are particularly outstanding. This is an essential book for all art glass libraries and will appeal to architects, builders, interior designers and all stained glass enthusiasts.

WINDOWS OF ELEGANCE by Glass Reflections Designers   80 pages   108 Color photographs   48 Drawings

This design studio portfolio contains over 150 designs for stained glass windows. The photographs and drawings are from the designer archive at Glass Reflections of Fort Lauderdale. The array of design styles include traditional, tropical, floral, beveled panels, modern abstracts, landscapes, and magnificent entryways. This book is indispensible in all art glass libraries and will appeal to architects, builders, interior designers and all stained glass enthusiasts

WINDOWS OF NORTH AMERICA a collection of Nine Glass Design Studios   80 pages   108 Color photographs   48 Drawings

You are invited to take a tour of nine renowned art glass studios located throughout the USA and across Canada. This book contains one of the most inspiring collections of designer glass ever assembled. Each studio is featured in an 8 page layout presenting color photographs of spectacular installations and artists proposals. This book will be a valued addition to all art glass libraries and is essential for architects, interior designers, glass artists and everyone who appreciates beautiful glass.

Wardell Publications

The Finest Quality
Books for
Discriminating
Stained Glass Artist

FULL SIZE
LAMPSHADE PATTERNS I
FOR MINI TO MEDIUM SIZED SHADES

22 PATTERNS FOR SWAG OR BASE
COLOR PHOTOGRAPH OF EACH COMPLETED
STEP BY STEP LESSONS — TRADE SECR

MORE
LAMPSHADE PATTERNS II
FOR 15" TO 22" DIAMETER SHADES

FULL-SIZE PATTERNS
FOR
11 UNIQUE DESIGNS
STEP-BY-STEP INSTRUCTIONS — LAMPFORMS NOT RE

DESIGNS FOR
BEVEL ART LAMPSHADES
by CHARLES KNAPP

29 FULL-SIZE PATTERNS
FOR 6" to 36" DIAMETER SHADES

COMPLETE STEP-BY-STEP GUIDE
TO LAMPSHADE CONSTRUCTION
Using over 50 how-to photographs

NORTHERN SHADES
25 FULL-SIZE PATTERNS FOR STAINED GLASS LAMPSHADES

25 LAMP PATTERNS FOR 8" TO 22" DIAMETER SHADES - STYLES INCLUDE:
MINI • INVERTED CEILING • WALL SCONCE • TABLE • SWAG
STEP-BY-STEP INSTRUCTIONS - LAMPFORMS NOT REQUIRED

CHARLES KNAPP
DESIGNS FOR LAMPS
PATTERNS FOR 18 SMALL TO MEDIUM SHAD

FULL-SIZE PATTERNS FOR SWAG & BASE LAMPSHADES
STEP-BY-STEP ASSEMBLY INSTRUCTIONS

LAMPWORKS
FULL-SIZE PATTERNS FOR STAINED GLASS LAMPSHA

CHARLES KNAPP   RANDY & JUDY WARDE

BRIAN EAGLE   LINDA

16 UNIQUE DESIGN STYLES FOR 10" TO 24" DIAMETER S
STEP-BY-STEP INSTRUCTIONS—LAMPFORMS NOT REQUIR

QUICK SUCCESS STAINED GLASS
A BEGINNER'S INSTRUCTION G

INTRODUCTION TO STAINED GLASS
A TEACHING MANUAL

A COMPLETE HOW-TO-DO STAINED GLASS MANUAL
INCLUDING FULL-SIZE PATTERNS FOR 17 PROJECTS

• WARDELL PUBLICATIONS • STUDIO DESIGNER SERIES •
Stained Glass
Windows of North America
Collection Three

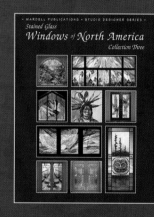

• WARDELL PUBLICATIONS • STUDIO DESIGNER SERIES •
Stained Glass
Windows of Elegance
Collection Two

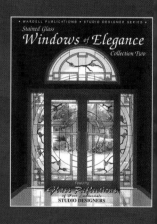

Featuring
Glass Reflections
of Fort Lauderdale
STUDIO DESIGNERS

• WARDELL PUBLICATIONS • STUDIO DESIGNER SERIES •
Stained Glass
Windows of Distinction
Collection One

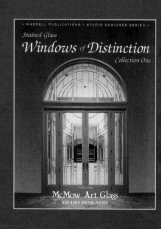

Featuring
McMow Art Glass
STUDIO DESIGNERS

32 FULL-SIZE FREE-FORM DESIGNS FOR
ART GLASS INSPIRATION
by SUE CANN

32 FULL-SIZE P
FOR
FREE-FORM
WINDOW LIG

STAINED GLASS
WALL DECORATIONS
PATTERNS FOR CLOCKS,
MIRRORS AND PICTURE FRAMES

DESIGNS FOR 29 COMPLETE PROJECT
STEP-BY-STEP INSTRUCTION

STAINED GLASS
CLOCK GALLERY

DESIGNS FOR
STEP-BY-STEP IN

Classic Alphabets
by Tammie Martin
FULL-SIZE ALPHABETS & NUMERALS

Welcome

SIX COMPLETE ALPHABETS IN THREE DIFFERENT STYLES

DETAILED TECHNIQUES FOR DESIGNING WITH LETTERS
22 DESIGN DRAWINGS AND 8 FULL-SIZE PROJECT PATTERNS

PATTERNS FOR
STAINED GLASS BOXES

DESIGNS FOR 34 COMPLETE PROJECT
STEP-BY-STEP INSTRUCTIONS

SECOND EDITION - REVISED & UPDATED
BEVEL WINDOW DESIGNS
PATTERNS, PHOTOS & DRAWINGS
FEATURING - BEVEL KING, CLUSTERS

OVER 100 DESIGN DRAWINGS
55 BEVEL KING, CLUSTER DESIGNS
INCLUDING 28 NEW BEVELED CLUSTERS
MANY NEW WINDOW PATTERN DRAWINGS
STEP-BY-STEP DRAWING TECHNIQUES

PATTERNS FOR
MIRRORS & FRAMES

PATTERNS FOR
TERRARIUMS & PLANTERS

DESIGNS FOR 30 COMPLETE PROJECTS
GUIDE TO SELECTION AND CARE OF PLANTS
STEP-BY-STEP INSTRUCTION

Email us at: wardellpub.aol.com
W.W.Web: http://www.thestorefinder.com/manufacturers/wardellhome.html

Studio Designer Series